D1243158

LAUGH OUT LOUD!
THE FUN ON THE FARM
JOKE BOOK

Sean Connolly

WINDMILL BOOKS

New York

Published in 2013 by Windmill Books, An Imprint of Rosen Publishing
29 East 21st Street, New York, NY 10010

First Edition

Editor: Joe Harris
Illustrations: Adam Clay (cover) and Dynamo Design (interiors)
Layout Design: Notion Design

Library of Congress Cataloging-in-Publication Data

Connolly, Sean. 1956–
  The fun on the farm joke book / by Sean Connolly. — 1st ed.
      p. cm. — (Laugh out loud)
  Includes index.
  ISBN 978-1-61533-644-9 (library binding) — ISBN 978-1-61533-654-8 (pbk.) —
  ISBN 978-1-61533-655-5 (6-pack)
  1. Agriculture—Juvenile humor. 2. Animals—Juvenile humor. 3. Farm life—Juvenile humor. 4. Riddles,
Juvenile. I. Title.
  PN6231.A44C55 2013
  808.88'2—dc23
                                      2012019528

Printed in China

CPSIA Compliance Information: Batch #AW3102WM: For Further Information contact Windmill Books, New York, New York at 1-866-478-0556
SL002422US

CONTENTS

Jokes..................................... 4

Glossary.................................. 32

Index..................................... 32

Further Reading........................... 32

Websites.................................. 32

FUN ON THE FARM

How do chicks get out of their shells?
They look for the eggs-it.

What's brown and sticky?
A stick!

What do you get it you cross a sheepdog and a fruit?
A melon-collie!

Teacher: Name five things that contain milk.
Pupil: Yogurt, cheese, and three cows!

What do you get when you cross a
rooster with a duck?
A bird that gets
up at the
quack of
dawn.

FUN ON THE FARM

What's a pig's
favorite ballet?
Swine Lake.

Teacher: How would
you hire a farm worker?
Pupil: Put a brick under
each leg.

What did the pig say when the
farmer grabbed him by the tail?
"That's the end of me."

Knock, knock!
Who's there?
Farmer.
Farmer who?
Farmer distance, your house looks much bigger!

What happened when the sheep pen broke?
The sheep had to use a pencil.

FUN ON THE FARM

Texan: On my uncle's ranch, cowboys round up cattle on horseback!
New Yorker: Wow! I didn't know cows could ride horses!

What did the baby corn say to the mom corn?
Where's my pop corn?

Where do horses and ponies live?
In the neigh-borhood.

Knock, knock!
Who's there?
Lass.
Lass who?
How long have you been a cowboy?

How do you make a chicken stew?
Keep it waiting for a couple of hours.

FUN ON THE FARM

What did the waiter say when the horse walked into the café?
"Why the long face?"

Where do horses stay in hotels?
The bridle suite.

Is chicken soup good for your health?
Not if you're the chicken!

What do you get if you cross a cow with a grass cutter?
A lawn mooer!

How do you make an apple puff?
Chase it around the kitchen.

FUN ON THE FARM

Did you hear about the scarecrow who won a gold medal?
He was out standing in his field.

What do you get if you cross a cow and a goat?
Butter from a butter!

What has lots of ears, but can't hear anything at all?
A cornfield.

What did the alien say to the plant?
"Take me to your weeder."

What did the farmer use to repair his overalls?
A cabbage patch.

How did the banana know
he was sick?
He wasn't peeling well.

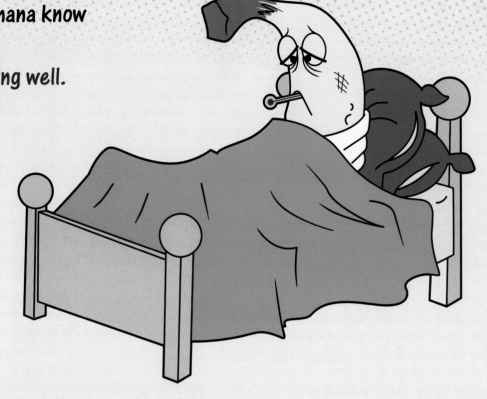

What do you
call a sheep
with no legs?
A cloud!

What do cows
eat for
breakfast?
Moosli!

Patient: Doctor, I feel as sick as a dog!
Doctor: I'll make an appointment for you to see a
veterinarian!

Where do sheep go on their summer vacation?
The Baaahaaamaaas!

Patient: Doctor, I feel like a goat!
Doctor: Really? And how are the kids?

What's green and sings in the vegetable patch?
Elvis Parsley.

Knock, knock!
Who's there?
Lettuce.
Lettuce who?
Lettuce in and you'll find out!

What did the horse say when it fell over?
"I've fallen and I can't giddy-up."

What do horses tell their children at bedtime?
Pony tales!

Patient: Doctor, what can I do to help me get to sleep?
Doctor: Have you tried counting sheep?
Patient: Yes, but then I have to wake up to drive home again!

FUN ON THE FARM

What do you give a sick pig?
Oinkment!

How did the musical farmer know which note to sing?
He used a pitchfork!

Why should you be careful where you step when it rains cats and dogs?
You could step in a poodle!

What do you call the wages paid to a gardener?
His celery!

What do you call a sleeping bull?
A bulldozer.

What do you get if you cross a chicken with a kangaroo?
Pouched eggs!

How did the pig with laryngitis feel?
Dis-gruntled.

Why do roosters curse all the time?
They are fowl-mouthed.

What do you call a car with its trunk full of eggs?
A hatchback.

What did the chicken say when it laid a square egg?
Owwww!

FUN ON THE FARM

What did the flamenco-
dancing farmer say to
his chickens?
"Oh, lay!"

Doctor, I feel like a dog!
How long have you felt
that way?
Since I was a puppy!

What do you get if you
feed gunpowder to a
chicken?
An egg-splosion!

Teacher: Define "defense."
Pupil: Something that runs
around de garden!

What did the farmer use to paint the new sty?
Pigment.

What do you call a factual TV show about sheep?
A flock-umentary!

Why did the goose cross the road?
To prove she wasn't chicken!

Patient: Doctor, I got trampled by a load of cows!
Doctor: So I herd!

What do you give a pony with a cold?
Cough stirrup!

Why should you never tell your secrets to a piglet?
Because they might squeal!

FUN ON THE FARM

How do alien farmers round up their sheep?
They use tractor beams!

What do you get when you cross a chicken and a fox?
Just the fox.

How can you cook turkey that really tickles the taste buds?
Leave the feathers on!

How many pigs do you need to make a smell?
A phew!

What do you call a cow with an out-of-date map?
Udderly lost!

Where do cows go for history lessons?
To a mooseum!

What's a pig's favorite fairy tale?
Slopping Beauty.

If a small duck is called a duckling, what do you call
a small pen?
An inkling!

Mother: You can't keep a pig in your bedroom—what about the terrible smell?
Child: Don't worry, he'll soon get used to it!

What do you get if you cross a donkey and Christmas?
Muletide greetings!

What do you call a dog with a bunch of roses?
A collie-flower!

Why did the farmer's dog keep chasing his tail?
He was trying to make ends meet.

How does a sheep finish a letter?
Sincerely ewes.

Why did the chicken cross the playground?
To get to the other slide!

What sort of jokes do chickens like best?
Corny ones!

What do you get if you cross a cow and a jogging machine?
A milk shake!

How many sheep does it take to make a woolen sweater?
I didn't know sheep could knit!

What grows down as it grows up?
A goose!

Why is that farmer setting fire to the plants in his field?
He's growing baked beans!

What do you call a man who keeps rabbits?
Warren!

FUN ON THE FARM

What says, "Moo, baa, woof, quack, meow, oink?"
A sheep that speaks foreign languages!

What do you get if you cross a cow with a camel?
Lumpy milkshakes!

Where do sheep get shorn?
At the baa-baas!

What do you call cattle thieves who wear pants covered with newspaper?
Rustlers!

How does your dog get into the house?
Through the labra-door!

FUN ON THE FARM

Why are bulls so noisy?
Because they each have two bullhorns.

What do you call a tale with a twist at the end?
A pigtail!

What do you call a Russian gardener?
Ivanhoe!

If April showers bring May flowers, what do May flowers bring?
Pilgrims!

How do hens dance?
Chick to chick!

What kind of jewelry do
vegetables wear?
Onion rings.

Why is it
hard to carry on
a conversation
with a goat?
Because
they're always
trying to butt in.

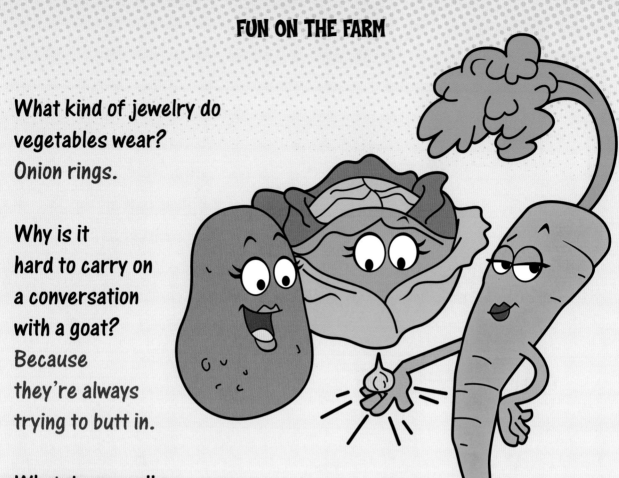

What do you call a
veterinarian with laryngitis?
A hoarse doctor.

What do penguins use to stay beautiful?
Cold cream.

What do you call a baby turkey?
A goblet.

What does it mean if you find a set of horse shoes?
A horse is walking around in his socks!

Why did the boy stand behind the horse?
He thought he might get a kick out of it.

What do you get from a forgetful cow?
Milk of amnesia.

What steps should you take if you see a bull charging toward you?
Big steps, and fast!

If you had fifteen cows and five goats, what would you have?
Plenty of milk!

FUN ON THE FARM

Why do pigs never go on vacation?
They prefer to sty at home.

What do you get if you cross a sheep with a porcupine?
An animal that knits its own sweaters.

What do you get from a pampered cow?
Milk that's spoiled.

What do you call a
pig with three eyes?
A piiig.

Why did the
chicken run out
onto the basketball
court?
Because the referee
whistled for a fowl!

FUN ON THE FARM

Young man, can you reach that package of beef from the top of the freezer?
No ma'am. The steaks are too high.

How does a bull buy his food?
He charges it.

What did the polite sheep say to his friend at the gate?
After ewe.

Have sheep ever flown?
No, but swine flu.

What did the duck say when she bought lipstick?
Put it on my bill!

FUN ON THE FARM

Why did the two pigs go
to Las Vegas for their vacation?
To play on the slop machines.

How did the
farmer find his
lost sheep?
He tractor
down.

Why does
Santa have
three
gardens?
So he can hoe hoe hoe.

What do you call a cow with only his two left legs?
Lean beef.

When do you know it's time for a farmer's family to go
to sleep?
When it's pasture bedtime.

What has five fingers and drives a tractor?
A farm hand.

What kind of animal goes OOM?
A cow walking backward!

What do you call cattle with a sense of humor?
Laughing stock.

Why did the farmer think someone was spying on him?
There were moles all over his field.

A cross between a cocker spaniel and a poodle is a called a cockapoo. So what do you call a cross between a cockapoo and a poodle?
A cock-a-doodle-do!

FUN ON THE FARM

What do you call a chicken crossing the road?
Poultry in motion.

Why did the pig's friends keep making fun of him when he invited them over for dinner?
It was a hog roast.

What is the best way to carve wood?
Whittle by whittle.

Why did the farmer plow his field with a steamroller?
He wanted to grow mashed potatoes.

Why do male deer need braces?
Because they have buck teeth.

FUN ON THE FARM

Why did the pig run away from the farm?
He felt that the others were taking him for grunted.

How do you make an apple turnover?
Roll it down a hill!

Why was the butcher
looking worried?
His job was at steak.

Two flies have landed
on the farmer's front
porch. Which one is the
actor?
The one on the screen!

What do you get if you
sit under a cow?
A pat on the head.

Why did the rooster get a tattoo?
He wanted to impress the chicks.

What do you get from an invisible cow?
Evaporated milk.

First cow in a field: "Moo."
Second cow: "Ohhh, I was going to say that!"

Why did the ram run over the cliff?
He didn't see the ewe turn!

What was the result when two silkworms had a race?
It ended in a tie.

What is a pig's favorite play?
Hamlet.

Did you hear about the magic tractor?
It drove down a lane and turned into a field.

What did the buffalo say to his son when he went away?
Bison!

Why didn't the piglets listen to their father?
Because he was an old boar.

Why did the fly fly away?
Because the spider spied her.

FUN ON THE FARM

Why did the pterodactyl cross the road?
Because chickens didn't exist back then.

Who judges the Farmyard Idol talent show?
Simon Cow-ell.

Which side of a chicken has the most feathers?
The outside.

Which horses aren't afraid of the dark?
Nightmares.

What do you get when you cross a cow with an octopus?
A cow that can milk itself.

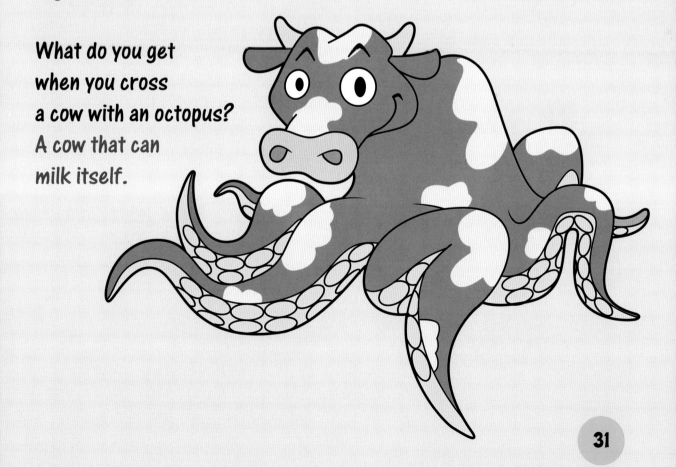

Glossary

amnesia (am-NEE-zhuh) memory loss

bullhorn (BUL-horn) a cone-shaped machine that makes your voice louder

laryngitis (leh-rin-JY-tis) an illness that might make you lose your voice

melancholy (MEH-len-kah-lee) a thoughtful sadness

pitch (PITCH) the highness or lowness of a musical note

swine flu (SWYN FLOO) an illness that affects pigs

whittle (WIH-tuhl) to carve small slices from a piece of wood

Further Reading

Chatterton, Martin. *What a Hoot!* New York: Kingfisher, 2005.

Dahl, Michael. *The Funny Farm: Jokes About Dogs, Cats, Ducks, Snakes, Bears, and Other Animals.* Mankato, MN: Picture Window Books, 2010.

Winter, Judy A. *Jokes About Animals.* Mankato, MN: Capstone Press, 2010.

Index

bulls 11, 20, 22, 24

chickens 6, 7, 12, 13, 14, 15, 17, 20, 23, 27, 29, 31

cows 4, 6, 7, 8, 9, 14, 15, 16, 18, 19, 20, 22, 23, 25, 26, 28, 29, 31

dogs 4, 9, 11, 13, 17, 19

farmers 5, 8, 11, 13, 15, 17, 18, 25, 26, 27, 28

goats 8, 9, 21, 22

horses 6, 7, 10, 22, 31

pigs 5, 11, 12, 13, 14, 15, 16, 20, 23, 24, 25, 27, 28, 30

sheep 5, 9, 10, 14, 15, 17, 18, 19, 23, 24, 25, 29

Websites

For Web resources related to the subject of this book, go to: www.windmillbooks.com/weblinks and select this book's title.